In It To Win It!

Charlette Denise Sutton

Copyright 2016
Charlette Denise Sutton

Published by Charlette Denise Sutton for My Words and Me
P.O. Box 114 Warsaw, NC 28398

Printed in the United States of America

All rights reserved. No part of this publication may be reproduced, transmitted, or stored in a retrieval system in any form - either mechanically, electronically, photocopy, recording, or other - except for short quotations in printed reviews, without the permission of the author. The author has warranted full ownership and/legal right to publish all materials in this book.

Editors:
Rebecca H. Judge
Jenny. B

Cover Design:
Jenny. B

Acknowledgements

To anyone who wants to be inspired,
this book is for you.
Life is meant to be treasured.
Honor it to the utmost!

Dedication Section

To my mom who taught me to believe and not give up;
To my dad who taught me to hope;
To my brother who taught me to love;
And to my sister who taught me to give.

Each life leaves behind a special message.
We who remain face the challenge of finding out what that message was……

Table of Contents

Acknowledgements iii
Dedication Section iv
Foreword vi
In It to Win It! 1
Choose Life 2
Conquer Your Mountains 4
Keep on Keeping On 5
Aspiring Towards Success 7
Dare to Believe 8
Images 9
The Entrepreneur 11
The Small Things 12
Each One, Teach One 14
One Word 16
Why I Teach 18
"I" Versus "You" 20
My Piano Keys 21
The Senior Citizen 23
I am Woman 25
A Great Man 27
Hero Without A Name 28
About the Author 30

Foreword

"Oops, you did it again!.... Oh no!.... Now, you're really in trouble!"

Breaking "rules" trapped the best of us. Sure, these rules had the potential to build character for they taught the difference between right and wrong. But, unfortunately, these same rules cloaked in phrases like "no", "don't do that", "you can't", and "that won't work", destroyed our ambitions. Somehow, we stopped seeing what COULD be done. We learned to fear taking chances. We dared not to think outside of the box. We feared that society would frown upon frivolous thoughts and behaviors. We grew accustomed to questioning our beliefs. Growing older, we learned to accept limitations. Yet, we felt the void left by an empty hopelessness.

In many of our minds, questions still linger. "Why haven't I achieved more?" "Why am I not doing what I love?"

"Why am I not fulfilled?"

We must look within ourselves to find the answers. Yet, so many fail to capture the "magic" that could solve that mystery.

That is where "In It to Win It" steps in. There's a challenge to finding those inner secrets that empower you and release you from all those mental traps. Why not rid yourself of the fear of rocking the boat or drowning in the "sea of life"? Instead, find out what keeps you afloat. Learn to swim, use your life jacket, or test taking a chance and, begin to walk on that "water"! Say hello to those shores of success waiting for you on the other side! Now, the next move is up to you. Jump in! Are you going to sit in the safe "boat" that is not moving in the direction you want to go? Or, are you going to take a chance on life and prove you are that undeterred survivor who can conquer any obstacle to reach your destination? Remember, while most people struggle to survive from day to day in the game of life, real winners know that we should be in it to win it!

*Addendum: A motivational speaker, in one of his videos, told how one day, he was beating his son continuously at a game of Connect Four. The son refused to call it quits. Only after winning the eleventh game did his son finally agree to go to bed. The speaker then asked his audience, "What if we were all like my son? What if no matter what happened to our dreams and goals daily, we were determined to stay in the race until we finally won!" Listen. Don't just play the game of life. Be **in it to win it**!*

In It to Win It!

Some people give their best; you don't have to ask.
Others do all they can to avoid any task.
But the secret to overcoming failure and grabbing success.
Is pressing on with determination when faced with a test.

Your life is a gift, don't waste it, live
If asked to do something, don't be afraid to give.
When faced with a circumstance, don't fear it, jump in it.
No time to back down now, we should be in it to win it!

Don't listen to naysayers that say it can't be done
And if you need a breakthrough, know God can send one.
Don't frown on hard work, it's your stepping stone.
By teaching you success and making it your own.

If you have faith and follow your master plan
When others say it won't happen, God says it can.
Your journey starts with one step, don't be afraid, begin it.
And never give in to failure, remember, you're in it to win it!

Choose Life

Some people walk around in fear and doubt.
As if they have nothing to rejoice about.
But I choose a new way of living each day.
By breathing the positive in all that I do and say.

You see I choose life, not death, you see.
Because I have a Living Savior who lives in me.
And nothing on earth can take this gift away.
No enemy can defeat me, come what may.

And I choose life, a gift so grand.
And unless you have it too, you won't quite understand.
How this life gives a joy and peace so complete,
That you want to share it with every single person that you meet.

I choose life, which is offered to you.
For God wants you to share in this experience too.
Letting the world know that through Calvary.
Death can be replaced by His Promise from Eternity!

" This day I call heaven and earth as witnesses against you that I have set before you, life and death, blessings and curses. Now choose life, so that you and your children may live"
Deuteronomy 30:19

Conquer Your Mountains

Conquer your mountain, reach for the sky;
Don't settle for low expectations, aim high.
Refuse to accept failure, when given chances, try.
And conquer your mountains.

Conquer your mountains, beat failure and win.
When faced with temptations to quit, don't falter, don't give in.
Your road to success starts when determination begins.
So, conquer your mountains.

Conquer your mountain, find a way to walk through.
If it takes the extra effort, climb over it if you have to.
With faith, demand that mountain to do what you want it to.
Yes, conquer those mountains.

Conquer your mountain in a way you do best.
With patience and persistence, you can stand above the rest
Your greatest motivation will be your most challenging test.
Just conquer your mountain.

Keep on Keeping On

My Steps are now slower, but as I look at my life,
O, the joy I have known.
And my heart continues to hold on to past memories,
That help me to keep on keeping on!

And during my life, I have crossed many paths,
And my loved ones tell me I'm never alone.
And I cherish those friendships that have come my way
And encourage me to keep on keeping on!

Another day is another chance for me to thank God
For in reality, I could have been gone.
Yet I'm still here for a reason, and I'm glad,
So, I'll just keep on keeping on!

I've made some mistakes, yet I call them lessons.
Because of my experiences, I have grown.
And now, I can use my life to help others
As I just keep on keeping on!

So, give up? No way! Throw in the towel?
Not today!
Because of the goodness that God has shown,
I can look forward to an even greater reward,
If I can just keep on keeping on!
Inspired by Willie M. Sutton

Aspiring Towards Success

You can be that "one" example,
You can be that shining star.
You can be the best "you" possible,
No matter who you are.

You can conquer any obstacle
And hold your head up high.
You can walk around with dignity,
With your face turned towards the sky.

You can overcome past failures,
Build strength to fight misery.
You can work towards a better tomorrow,
And go places you'd like to see.

In this world of opportunity,
It's easy if you understand,
Just act on what you believe in;
Success yields to your command!

Dare to Believe

I dare to dream. I dare to believe.
I dare to take a chance so that I can achieve.
I will say I can and know that it's true.
That I can make it happen if I want to.

Images

On the outside, I look pulled together.
On the inside, I'm falling apart.
On the outside, it appears that I've finished.
Inside, I ask, "Where do I start?"
On the outside, I look as good as new.
On the inside, I'm rugged and worn.
Outwardly, I appear mighty strong.
Inwardly, just tossed and torn.
Outwardly, I say, "I don't care."
Inwardly, it's eating me up inside.
Outwardly, it's easy for me to "cope".
Inside, I wonder, "Will I survive?"
Some days I say, "What's love got to do with it?"
Truth be told, it means everything to me.
To others, I'd vow to pay any price for success.
To myself, "I'm wishing it was free."
How long must I hide who am?
As if everything is okay?
Long enough to avoid the rejection
Of you not liking me "that way."

"Image is everything."
Sprite

Note from author: This poem is not intended to be depressing but to let everyone know that each of us, to some extent, have insecurities that make us afraid of letting the world know who the "real" person inside of us is…

The Entrepreneur

What a revelation. How wonderful it would be,
If I could turn what was just a dream into reality.
How empowering to acknowledge, and yet so divine.
To work for a company knowing that company was mine.

What an impact it would make to finally realize
What was once just an idea in my head, growing right before my eyes.
And seeing what I had to offer impacting others in some way,
With the potential to affect thousands, maybe millions someday.

And while making money is one of those things that I dream of,
I'd cherish more being able to work while doing what I love.
Calling the shots, making the decisions, I would be free.
So, I'll continue to cherish the entrepreneurial spirit in me!

The Small Things

Many strive to achieve great things
And feel like failures if they don't.
So even if you ask them to stay committed,
They may try to, but they won't.
But greatness comes not by being seen
Or even by making the news.
But, instead, by improving circumstances
By the actions that we choose.
So, it's not so much of the big things
But the small ones that go far.
In making the world a better place
No matter where you are.
So, strive to do your very best
And join with others who believe
In the relentless power of unity
And, the things that it can achieve.
And work at making a difference
By doing your "little bit".
And others will also be inspired
Because your heart is in it!

Inspired by the theme, "If Many Do Little, We Can Do Much" by Mrs. Lillie. Sanders, Magnolia, NC

Each One, Teach One

You may not reach a million people, but you can still reach some.
It begins with a phrase as simple as this, "Each one, teach one."
Life has its ups and downs, but remember this important fact,
Happiness may come by receiving things, but joy comes in giving back!

You don't need extensive education, not even an extravagant degree.
Knowledge expands when I help you, and, in return, you reach out to me.
With things fighting for our attention and so little time at hand,
Remember, it only takes an hour, a minute, a second to understand.

Tell others about our history; something we all need to know.
Where we've come from gives us direction on where we need to go.
Teach someone to deal with their emotions and express how they feel.
Prove to them there is a difference between what is fictional and real.

The world is full of people who hope to one day read.
Teach them a letter, a sound, a word, a listening ear is all they need!
There is so much that you can tell someone about the world out there.
By taking the time to give, encourage, and show others that you care.

We can leave the world a better place and look proudly at what we've done.
If we all succumb to the simple vision, "Each one, teach one!"

One Word

If I could leave behind some wisdom and instill some hope in you,
I would remind everyone precisely what one word can do.
One word can lift a sorrow; it can mend a broken heart.
One word can instill determination and encourage a brand new start.

One word can offer peace where there was once despair.
For one word can move a selfish heart to reach out and share.
One word can offer new direction where there was once no hope.
One word can build the esteem of another in order that they might cope.

One word can move millions; one word can win a race.
One word can instill in you a peace offered only by God's grace.
One word can lift the guilt you feel even if you've done wrong.

And one word can lead to a line, a verse, and eventually a song!

Why I Teach

People ask me why I teach.
Is it the lives that I touch or the souls that I reach?
Is it because of the knowledge that I'm willing to share?
Or is it the chances I'm given to show others that I care?

Is it because I get to play an incredible part?
Of giving someone the power to make a new start.
And if there is a concept that someone doesn't understand,
Are they more able to grasp its meaning with my helping hand?

People ask me why I teach and to this very day,
I can't explain the power of knowing I've shown someone else the way.
Each time that I see a student that I've helped to succeed
I remember the times I pushed him or her when there was a need.

When someone would come before me with excuses to give up,

I'd keep them in the race by saying, "You've got a point, but..."
And although other professions could give me more financially,
No monetary gain can replace the joy that teaching brings to me.

The greatest fulfillment of all is when I realize
That I've made a difference and the student's "thank you" is written in their eyes!

Inspired by my many years of being a nursing assistant instructor.

"I" Versus "You"

No big "I" in the game of life and in exchange, there's no little "you".
For who's to say my goal or mission is more important than what you do?
For mere achievement and recognition does not define one's worth.
And no one else can fulfill the purpose of why you were sent down to earth.

So why should I play down your importance by saying that you don't count?
And why so much concern about what you have, regardless of the amount?
Making you feel like the loser doesn't mean that I win.
For true value is not what we see outwardly, but rather what lies within.

My Piano Keys

I love playing my piano but the essence of its beauty to me
Is that eighty-eight keys come together as one to form a perfect harmony.
No one note is shouting, "I'm superior!" or "Look here, I'm the best!"
But instead, they intrinsically join in together to blend in with all the rest.
For each note knows that during a song, the strength of its sound
Is magnified all the more because the other notes are around.
Oh, if people were like these keys and lived in harmony,
Imagine the songs the world could produce. How beautiful they would be!
Like the music of Beethoven and Bach, we'd hear a heartfelt symphony,
The world could produce a work of art that would last through eternity.
These keys blending together in chords, scales, and arpeggios,

Remind me of people intertwining their hearts to sooth a million souls.
Stevie Wonder and Paul McCartney proved in "Ebony and Ivory",
That alone, we produce one sound; but joined together, we're a melody!

The Senior Citizen

I'm not just older but better, better in every way
Because those things that once were wrong, I made right yesterday.

I'm not just older but wiser, much wiser than before
And nothing, can take away the wisdom that I now have in store.

I'm not just older but more patient, for I know what's important now;
I take the time to enjoy life and fulfill my purpose each hour.

I'm not just older but richer, though many don't understand
That the wealth I have is not earthly but will follow me to Glory land.

I'm not just older but closer, closer to that great day
When all my cares will be memories and all pain will be washed away.

So, excuse me if my getting older does not weigh me down
And that I find peace in knowing that one day I won't be around.

For I know in this great circle of life, everything that I've gone through
Has prepared the way for someone else like me to face this journey too!

I am Woman

When you look this way, what do you see?
Can you envision the beauty that lies within me?
Or the determination that exudes from my face?
And the way that I walk around with such grace?

These eyes that have transported so many tears.
This smile that lingers despite my cares and fears.
Do you see the joy that I carry with me deep inside?
As I chase my dreams with destiny that won't be denied.

If you look deep enough, I'll tell you what you'll see;
A woman who'll move mountains in her struggle to be free.
A woman of substance, a woman of the earth,
Fighting to be recognized for all that she is worth

A woman who won't be defined by anyone else.
A woman who sets standards just by being herself.
One who'll be an example that others can live up to

And holds onto the motto, "To thine own self be true."

So, we take this month of March in order to recognize
The woman who takes the step to change others' lives.
And we celebrate the women of our future, present, and past,
Ones who are unforgettable and leave impressions that last

So, if you know a special woman, one that makes you proud,
Let the world know her value to you by shouting it out loud.
And even though this March celebration comes just once a year,
Let her know that each day she's special just because she is here.

A Great Man

Some people perceive you as great according to your fortune and fame.
Others say value is placed on you by titles attached to your name.
Some feel it takes an important job, a good organization will even do,
Or say whatever needs to be said when it comes to defining you.

But true power comes not in building a name, but in coming to realize
That we leave the world a much better place by touching other's lives.
And when many give up or walk away, true greatness says, "I will
Make a difference in the lives of others by showing a love that's real."

Hero Without A Name

They're not doing it for power or glory,
They're not tempted by fortune or fame.
They just feel compelled to help someone.
They're a "hero" without a name.

You won't see them grace a magazine cover.
They're not part of the popularity game.
They only want to make a difference.
A true "hero" without a name.

Many times, when you need someone in life,
They'll ask you, "What's in it for me."
Many want shrines built in their honor
So they can go down in history.

But the greatest act of giving
Asks for nothing in return.
We say it's more blessed to give than to receive,
But too many still haven't learned.

Real heroes carry no great titles
In history books, they may have no part.
But true heroes are the ones that we never forget
For their kindness, lives on within our hearts.

About the Author

Denise Sutton, a registered psychiatric nurse for twenty-two plus years, lives and works in eastern North Carolina. She enjoys writing poetry and inspirational themed titles. She began publishing in 2003 with the poetry book, <u>My Words and Me</u>. She later published <u>Do You Know Him?</u> (2005) and <u>Seizing Opportunities That Propel You Forward</u> (2009). In addition to this, she produced several musical CD's in which she was the songwriter. These included "Words Can't Tell" (2005), "What's in It For God?" (2005), "Decade of Hope" (2011), and "Wait" (2019). She also acted as the chief writer and editor of Sarah Refuge, Inc's collective book of poems and informative material on domestic abuse entitled, <u>Breaking the Silence: Victims No More</u> (2013) and her local sorority's chapter history book entitled <u>Chi Iota Omega Chapter Pearls of Timeless Service</u> (2014). In the past, Denise has coordinated community colleges publishing seminars and has sponsored community poetry readings. You may learn more about her works at <u>www.mywordsandme.com</u> or www.lyricalrainmaker.com. She may be reached at mywordsandme@yahoo.com.

www.ingramcontent.com/pod-product-compliance
Lightning Source LLC
Chambersburg PA
CBHW070756050426
42452CB00010B/1866